Earth in Action

Wildfires

by Matt Doeden

Consulting Editor: Gail Saunders-Smith, PhD

Consultant: Susan L. Cutter, PhD
Carolina Distinguished Professor and Director,
Hazards & Vulnerability Research Institute
Department of Geography, University of South Carolina

CAPSTONE PRESS
a capstone imprint

Pebble Plus is published by Capstone Press,
151 Good Counsel Drive, P.O. Box 669, Mankato, Minnesota 56002.
www.capstonepress.com

092009
005618CGS10

Library of Congress Cataloging-in-Publication Data
Doeden, Matt.
    Wildfires / by Matt Doeden.
    p. cm. — (Pebble plus. Earth in action)
    Includes bibliographical references and index.
    Summary: "Describes wildfires, how they occur, and the ways people can stay safe" — Provided by publisher.
    ISBN 978-1-4296-4719-9 (library binding)
    1. Wildfires — Juvenile literature. I. Title.
SD421.23.D64 2010
363.37'9 — dc22   2009036869

Editorial Credits

Erika L. Shores, editor; Heidi Thompson, designer; Jo Miller, media researcher; Eric Mankse, production specialist

Photo Credits

FEMA News Photo/Andrea Booher, 1, 19
Getty Images Inc./David McNew, 21; The Image Bank/Jose Luis Pelaez, 15; Justin Sullivan, 13; Milos Bicanski, 17;
    Photographer's Choice/Kathy Quirk-Syvertsen, 9; Stone/Bryce Duffy, 11
iStockphoto/David Parsons, cover
Shutterstock/Denis and Yulia Pogostins, 7; Peter Weber, 5

Note to Parents and Teachers

The Earth in Action set supports national science standards related to earth science. This
book describes and illustrates wildfires. The images support early readers in understanding
the text. The repetition of words and phrases helps early readers learn new words. This book
also introduces early readers to subject-specific vocabulary words, which are defined in
the Glossary section. Early readers may need assistance to read some words and to use the
Table of Contents, Glossary, Read More, Internet Sites, and Index sections of the book.

Table of Contents

What Is a Wildfire?

A wildfire is an outdoor fire that burns out of control. Wildfires burn grass, trees, homes, and everything else in their paths.

Most wildfires happen when
grass, trees, and soil are dry.
Wildfires usually happen
in summer and fall.

What Causes Wildfires?

People cause most wildfires.

Some fires start when a campfire

is left alone to burn out.

Other times people start fires

on purpose.

Lightning can start fires.
Lightning may strike
dry trees or plants.
Strong winds make
wildfires spread quickly.

Wildfire Safety

Wildfires are dangerous.

People should leave the area

if a fire is near their home.

Leaving is called evacuating.

Sometimes people cannot
get away in time.
At home, they should
stay away from outside walls
and windows.

People outside need to avoid heat and smoke. They should cover their mouth and nose. They should find a place with few plants and lay down.

Fighting Wildfires

Firefighters try to stop wildfires.

They use axes to clear plants

so the fire cannot spread.

Firefighters pour water
and chemicals on wildfires.
Firefighters work to keep
people and their homes safe.

Glossary

chemical — a substance made for a specific purpose

evacuate — to get away from danger by leaving an area

firefighter — a person who is trained to put out fires or stop them from spreading

lightning — a strong burst of electricity that passes between a cloud and the ground

Read More

Hamilton, John. *Wildfires.* Nature's Fury. Edina, Minn.: Abdo, 2006.

Menon, Sujatha. *Fire & Flood.* Wild Nature. New York: PowerKids Press, 2008.

Peppas, Lynn. *Wildfire Alert!* Disaster Alert! New York: Crabtree, 2004.

Internet Sites

FactHound offers a safe, fun way to find Internet sites related to this book. All of the sites on FactHound have been researched by our staff.

Here's all you do:

Visit *www.facthound.com*

FactHound will fetch the best sites for you!

Index

Word Count: 174

Grade: 1

Early-Intervention Level: 15